Lorn

Souls

Lorn

Souls

Dejah Freeman

Cover Art by Onur Burc

IVY CHAFIN
PRESS

Names: Freeman, Dejah, author.

Title: Lorn Souls / Dejah Freeman.

Editor: Jessica Berry
Cover design by Onur Burc
Description: Second edition. | Columbus, Ohio, 2025.

Identifiers: ISBN 979-8-9889632-0-2 (hardback)
ISBN 979-8-9889632-1-9 (paperback)

Ivy Chafin Press
Columbus, Ohio
www.ivychafinpress.com

Other Titles by Dejah Freeman

Dedication

I would like to thank God for, honestly, bringing me this far. He has carried me through so much and I am grateful. He has been blessing me my entire life and I wish there were more ways to express my gratitude. Without Him, I wouldn't be here today.

I would also love to give a huge thank you to all my family, friends, professors, and coworkers for their continuously loving support. I am so appreciative to have you all in my corner. Thank you for constantly motivating me. I love each of you!

Also, a big shoutout to my late grandpa. Rest in peace, twin!

Just like my thoughts, these poems are everywhere.

Sometimes, there's no reward for being a good person
Just drainage, tears and questions

I want so desperately to forget you
To wish you were just a memory I could think about and
continue with my day
But that isn't the case
You are the memory that brings tears to my eyes
during my happiest moments
The memory, so surreal I can still feel the touch of your
fingertips
Even when you're not touching me
The memory that replays in my head, constantly
invading my private thoughts
You are the memory that never leaves

It's not easy to let go of someone you love
This isn't a "love you"
This is an "*I* love you"
When you love someone, you're captivated by their
demeanor, actions, mindset, everything
You look deep into their soul and analyze why you love
them
What it is that makes you crave them
And this…this is why love is dangerous

I've cried so many years, enough to create an eighth sea
I don't cry tears of joy
I cry tears of suffrage
Tears of pain
Tears of sadness
Tears of misery
In each tear is a reason
And with each teardrop
I am slowly dying

I don't know what's worse
The heartbreak, or still having hope

I want to know what it feels like to be empty
Free of worries
Free of thoughts
Free of anxiety
It's getting repetitive to wake up and have the same
thoughts over and over again
Why can't I ever think positive thoughts
Why can't I ever tell myself everything will be alright
with reassurance
Instead, I overthink and worry, fueling my anxiety
I want to know what it's like to be completely happy
To wake up knowing you have a purpose and aspirations
to fulfill
I want to know what it's like, knowing you're pretty
without second-guessing yourself and looking in the
mirror for flaws

I'm difficult, but I'm a good one
People often take my heart for granted
I get happy for two seconds, then it fades away
The kind of happiness that comes, then leaves you stranded
I walk around like everything is fine
Knowing deep, deep down I'm broken
It's kind of hard to choose between my mind and my heart
When my mind is the one that reveals the truth
I sometimes don't make the best decisions
And if I do, they come back to haunt me
It's a constant battle between my thoughts and
a battle I constantly fight
I don't know when this feeling will end
Or if the pain will ever truly stop
Waking up from pre-sadness is getting tiring
As I continue to sit, overthink, and rot

I remember holding your hand
as you led me through the darkness
Trusting you to guide me
Expecting you to protect me
When I look back,
I crumble at the thought
of just how foolish I was
Thinking it would be you
to lead me down the path of love
The most dangerous thing I've ever done
was trust a man who walks in darkness
holding the hand of someone he claims to love
with his eyes completely shut

It's not *the* sad truth, it's *my* sad truth

Depression is being hopeful for rainbows and clear skies
but expecting rainy, stormy days
Depression is smiling during the day
but endlessly crying at night
Saying, "I'm fine"
When you really feel like the suffering won't end
Making sure everyone else is straight
but drowning in your own tears
Wanting help
but not wanting to ask
A dark bubble called life
And the bubble just won't pop
Fighting battles with your thoughts
And losing the war each time
Wanting to be alone
But hating the fact we feel alone
Depression is dark
A room with no light
A room with no door

Sometimes, I fear I'll never be beautiful enough,
or whole enough for another being
That I won't amount to what I'm destined to be
Or that I'll die before my dreams are set amid
That I won't look the part, but I fail to realize
that how others perceive me is not my problem
Yet, what I'm being perceived on is faulty
I worry my fears are approaching through the winds
And they will soon bound and shackle me
as if the sanctuary of my own thoughts weren't hellacious
enough
What if I never become the writer I always hoped to be
Or that, somehow, I write my own failure
Oh, how my worries trouble me daily
And leave tears that become implements of my pain

You men are never satisfied with the beauty of just one
Just having one lover
Just having one sexual attraction
Just having one taste
You prefer things…women…in multiples
And the moment you become tired of her,
you choose the next one
It's always good to have at least one backup plan
You make that one woman feel special
Then the next
Then the woman after that one
But I want to know what it feels like, for once
To be number one in a man's life
I guess that'll only happen in one's dream

I've ruined my happiness so many times
Too afraid to show emotion that, when I do, it's too late
Too afraid to get attached because they'll leave anyway
I know what it's like to lose all hope
Don't ever try to tell me I don't know what being unhappy
feels like

I'm the kind to listen to your story
while no one else is listening
I'm the kind to mend your heart
while mine is completely broken
I'm the kind to give you strength
when all my strength is gone
When everyone leaves your side,
I'll be the last one remaining
I'll wipe your tears away and dry your face
I'll pray for you before I pray for myself
I'm the kind to heal others,
while no one dares to try to heal me

I'm too nice of a person
I let those who break me back in
I give them all my attention
Put their needs before mine
Treat them as if they never hurt me
But I'll never forget what they did
And how I was left feeling
And in the back of my mind,
the pain is always present
But I push it aside
to show them I no longer care

I already lost myself once
I refuse to lose myself *again*

I stopped feeling a long time ago
So I'm sorry if I barely show emotion
I broke that function a long time ago
With the help of many, many others

I hope whenever love decides to enter my life
that I'm ready for it
The genuine love I daydream about
The type of love that barely exists nowadays
But we're the reason people still believe
Part of me is scared I'll be the one to ruin it
I'll push him away with my trust issues
Or my sadness will place itself before him
Maybe he'll wake up one day
and decide I'm not what he wants anymore
And just like that,
my world will collapse
Because every time I let someone in,
They show me I should have kept the door shut

It's challenging for me to give up on someone
I will give you a million chances
before I come to my senses and learn that you're no longer good
for me
I will find every excuse in the book to keep you in my life
I don't know why
Maybe it's because I have a benign heart
Or maybe because I'm easily taken advantage of
Whatever it is, it always seems to hurt me in the end
And no matter how much I try to expunge people,
I still welcome them back with open arms

I believed I was happy
I believed I felt complete
Yet, I lived, but wasn't alive
And that's when I wasn't me
I realized, I was living for others
Not necessarily living for myself
And, when you do that, you're not living at all
A human being occupying oxygen
An individual obtaining spaces
However, those tears, they were mine
The one thing I had to myself
The only thing I knew how to do
The salty, clear fluid, dropping from my eyes
In the dark is when they released
In the light is when they hid
Regardless of the matter,
I still have the fluid dropping from my eyes

Is it possible to be soulmates
even with our lost souls

I've learned the extremely hard way that many things
can't be reversed
You can't pause time, or rewind it, nor fast forward it
You can't erase the emotions you've felt
Or take back the tears you've cried
Nor take back the words someone said to you
You can only take those words and put them behind you
But it's difficult to forget how those words made you
feel
How those words cut skin, deep into your soul
How someone had the capability to break you with
words
Words they don't regret saying
Words they'll never take back
And I learned this at a young age
That people will destroy you with no remorse attached
And, yes, it hurts so bad
But I took those words and ate them
And swallowed the tears that burned my throat
Because I learned the hard way that
some things can't be reversed

I can't quite put my finger on it
And I can no longer hide the fact I'm being eaten alive
Perhaps by my thoughts
Perhaps by life itself
And I very much wonder
Why do I always write the most when I'm sad
Why don't words flow when the tears don't
Maybe the universe likes me best when I'm sad
Life has a funny way of showing its true colors
But these colors are so dark
And I've gotten used to the darkness
The slower breaths
The slower heartbeats
The throbbing in my head
I'm losing myself again

Take me back to when I didn't know love
I knew Barbies, I knew baby dolls, I knew cartoons
But I didn't know love
Take me back to who I was before the heartbreak
The warmth, the smiles, the innocence
Not the indurative of my heart
Maybe my smile was real back then
Not one that takes every muscle in my body
And even then,
it still feels forced
I yearn for who I was
Before my happiness was taken away
at the dismissal of another being
Too pure, I let my guard down
Created an unwanted monster
Because whatever is left is far from who I was

I yearn to be saved
To be heard just for once
For someone to hug me
before I explode
Because I want to give up
And I can't keep faking this smile
I try so hard to feel alive,
for even a second
And a second is all I get
But who will hug me
Whose arms will release my tears
without mocking me
Without the sympathetic grin
Without throwing it in my face
As I thought,
no one
I don't have the ability to hug myself
But if I did,
I'd hug myself so hard
I'd try to stop my breathing

I ignored all the signs
Red flags don't seem to mean anything
when you're color blind
Right there in my face
Shouting at me to leave you from the moment we met
Shouting does no good when you're deaf
All the names you called me
The bruises on my skin turning purple and blue
None of them ever seemed to hurt
when I lost the ability to feel a long time ago

Sometimes, I wish
 were given another opportunity at life
So many things I would do differently
So many people I would avoid meeting
Many emotions I would never engage in
But sadly,
life doesn't work out that way
One life
One chance
But in my dreams,
I'm given multiple
I guess that's why I live in my dreams

I want to break free from everyone
All people seem to do is bring me
Tears
Stress
Disappointment
I wish for everyone to forget I existed
Cause when I don't talk to people,
I'm at peace, with somewhat of a clear mind
In my natural quiet state,
around people, I'm anxious
Always have to be alert
Watch out for the knavery around me
I don't like being like that
I would, without a doubt, choose to be alone
than to be wrapped in the presence of others
I don't think I was created to like people
Only to tolerate them…for the time being

I feel the people who have
dug themselves out of depression
deserve more than a pat on the back
That shit is one of the hardest tasks given to mankind
Almost feels impossible
and hard for one to do on their own

I think, sometimes, I feel more than I should
And sometimes, I hide the sadness way
beneath the visible layers
Tucked away under the epidermis
to where it finds its way into my cells
And my body becomes the sadness
I walk with the sadness
Talk with the sadness
Inhale and exhale complete sadness
And without it, it's like my body can't function

Maybe I'm just hoping
for a romantic fairytale I'm sure won't happen
Oh, but how I wish
to watch the sunset with my love
To dine in small diners at 10 p.m.
Then we stay in the car and chat about life
like we had just met hours before
How he'll notice my hair frizzing in the wind,
then pat it down gently
After, he'll place a loving kiss on my lips
I hope to bake a strawberry cake with my love
Then put strawberry icing on his lips
Turn on one of our favorite horror movies
Cuddle under the blankets
Light every candle in the room
But yeah, maybe I'm just hoping

I say I want to die
as a means to escape
But in actuality,
I'm beyond terrified of death
I don't know what's up there
And finding out terrifies me more than anything
My heart races
And I stare off into space
Scared of the fact I will die one day
Not sure of where my soul will wander
I wish I weren't so scared
Instead of living my life,
I'm too busy fearing my own death

I learned through a lot of self-healing, reflection and talks with God that a response isn't always needed. Despite how much I would like to speak on how I feel, it's best I let God handle most situations. Not only for the sake of my sanity, but for peace of mind. I had to let certain things be or else I was going to drive myself crazy. Missed meals, missed hours of sleep. All over things out of my control. I hate letting the worst people get the best of me. People drained me, and it was messing me up mentally. Fixing everyone when I, myself, was completely broken. Putting Band-Aids on my wounds while giving full treatment to others. I've never been the type to put myself first, but damn, maybe I should consider it. Maybe I'd be happier if I tuned everyone out and acted like they didn't exist. Or maybe I'd be happier if they acted like *I* didn't exist.

The purity of love seems like something I will only
imagine
I'm too busy being directed by horny boys
with no invitation inside of me,
Yet one keeps
finding himself there
I can't say it's love that prompts me to do it
Perhaps lust, from both ends
Love between us is only a word
We've been hurt far too many times
to believe we have the capability to love
We look at each other like natural born sinners
examining what we believe seems to have potential
But we look away quickly
Because love is something we have tucked away
far beneath our skin, until the day we die

I fear attachment
The thought of getting close to someone
just for them to leave less than a year later
brings tears to my eyes
It's always the people you expect to stay
who are always the first to leave
After a while, I became used to it
These new friendships have potential
But the little voice in the back of my mind
reminds me, they won't last
Don't get attached to an empty vessel
Don't show them your closed wounds
They'll take your pain and make a mockery of it
And for the wounds they caused,
close them like the other ones
Cause we know there's more to come

I will never understand why those
with the good hearts never have peace
Why they go out of their way to fulfill
but their ends never meet
Why they wipe the tears of others
Because they know the pain is urgent
Why they never feel like someone's happiness
Instead, they're stuck feeling like the burden
They feel like the world is on their shoulders
And it's slowing, crashing down
No one to vent to or wipe their tears,
despite there being many people around
But in the end, things get better
Because God hears their cries
No more pain, no more tears
No more sadness or broken ties

Love has a way of manipulating me
Inviting its presence in without a knock
Then exiting the room, right when I need it most
Obtaining authority over my benign heart
And allowing savages to swallow it whole
Until there is no heart left
I will never understand why love treats me so
When all I ever wanted was to be loved
And to love those who I adore properly
To not view the madness of love
Or all of the insecurities it imprisons
But to bathe in the essence of it

I don't trust people
because their intentions are never pure
I don't trust people
because they wake up with different feelings
And when I did put my trust in people,
they gave me more than enough reasons
why I shouldn't
Because they're not as solid as they claim
And not as honest as they say they are
How they act like they care about you
but it is only an act
How trust sometimes is the reason
two individuals separate
Because neither trusted each other enough

With a heart that feels too much,
I could never be heartless
No matter how many times
I try to let things go,
to just let them be
My heart doesn't allow that kind of power
I feel what no longer needs to be felt
Cry tears I thought had dried
And dream scenarios that are too unrealistic
Though my heart is strong,
it's soft
I feel things, too
I just feel them a little too much

There were times when I didn't care
because I knew not caring meant not getting hurt
How I would brush off things that bothered me
and quickly wipe away preforming tears
But when it comes to certain people,
the satisfaction of not caring goes away
Because as much as you hate to admit,
you care about the things they do
Which means inviting the hurt
And allowing the tears to fall as they quickly form
and it's like I can't win
Because when I didn't care, I got hurt
And when I did care, I was broken

Life is so short
And there's so much I still have yet to do
Going to sleep, fearing I won't wake up
But waking up and not living as if it were my last
People I haven't conversed with
Memories that still need to be made
Adventures I still haven't risked

I often think about the past
The memories tend to haunt me
After all this time,
my heart still hurts
It still cries in the late nights
And I want to forget you
so badly it hurts
I really don't know why I can't
Why my heart won't let me
So I suffer
I reminisce
Then I suffer some more

In some ways, I believe we're all hurting
Untold stories hidden in tattoos
Tears dropping and being rolled into our blunts
Unreleased anger being swallowed down our throats
The pain is too impalpable
So we allow the alcohol to wash it down
Crying silently, hoping someone is close enough to hear
Secretly feeling like they won't care
Because what is an "It will be okay" gonna do
After all, I believe we're all *Lorn Souls*

People just don't understand how much they drain me
Every ounce of hope
Every pint of happiness
leaves the moment I let them in
And every time,
every single time
I think each individual is different
Maybe *this* one has something different to offer
I'm wrong, every time
And it's tiring
It's frustrating
The anticipation of meeting someone has run its
course
And quite frankly, it's a track I never want to run on
again

It sucks to be so understanding
To try to see a situation from every perspective
Putting yourself in someone's shoes
despite if they're too big or too small
And yet,
no one really understands you
Or even tries to, for that matter
You're a big question mark
And many people think they have you figured out
Therefore, they won't have to try
But they're wrong
They don't validate your feelings
Or understand that you speak about how you feel
Or how you meant it in a subtle tone, but it came out
harsh
Maybe you're not meant to be understood
But it'd be nice to see how that feels for once

I feel like I was placed on Earth
To give love
To spread love
To embrace love
To reminisce about love
But never to receive it
To actually experience the genuine feeling of love
To actually say someone loves me
And although I don't mind,
cause everyone needs love in their life,
I wonder who will give me love besides myself
Who will give me a reason to believe in love
To be thankful love exists

I love you so much, and it hurts
It burns a hole in my chest
Swells my throat as if a rope is being tied around it.
Removes whatever words out of my mouth
The same mouth that once said, "I love you"

You know how to really mess someone up for life
Say you love them
Then leave

I just want you to hold me in your arms
as I endlessly sob
And reassure me everything will be okay

But that's not your place anymore
You comfort *her* when she sobs
Now I sob even harder

And alone

It was when I was crying—
you were the first person I wanted to call
and the only person I wanted to hold me
that I knew
I Loved You

I've been hurt so much
I've become numb to the pain
You can't hurt someone
who can no longer feel

I feel myself changing
Activities no longer excite me
I don't want to be bothered by people
I feel consummate when I'm isolated
I'm scared
What am I becoming

I learned to take the hurt and swallow it
No one was listening anyway.

One minute, I'm doing fine. I feel there is hope for the future. I become optimistic, and I can't wait for blessings to come my way. I feel like my life is going to work out in the end and God will make a way

Then, two seconds later,

I'm crying myself to sleep. Wondering when my life will get better and why it is that everyone else is receiving blessings and I'm still stuck feeling hopeless. I wonder why things in the past happened and reflect on how damaged I am, and who could ever love a damaged person

When you feel like giving up,
remember, God woke you up this morning
You deserve to be alive
You deserve to be happy
And if you have to obtain that happiness alone,
then you do just that

I want a fairy-tale love
Where we fall in love and never fall out
Move in together
Start a family
Connect mentally and physically
But then I remembered
that only happens in fairy tales

You have had numerous heartbreaks
Ones you thought you would never overcome
Times when you would lay awake at night,
wondering if you're deserving of love
And despite what you think you are,
you deserve that person
That someone who thanks God every day because
He placed you in their life
And you will meet that someone
Don't give up now
Your blessing is around the corner

I doubt you're hurting
In no way, shape, or form has it been shown that you are
You've continued with life
You've found someone else
You go about your day as if I never existed

Meanwhile,

I'm hurting enough for the both of us
I may not show it, but I'm deeply broken
I can't move on with life so easily
I don't think I'll find anyone else
I know you exist because it's too hard to forget you

With life comes pleasure, pain, and healing
You decide which one you want to end in

When I look into your eyes,
I don't see the man I fell in love with
Instead,
I see the man who fell out of love with me

I'm not even living
It's more of existing

If it hurts, then it hurts
Don't be ashamed to cry about it
Don't be afraid to vent about it
Don't bottle it up
You'll be come angrier
Let it out
Then, pray about it

You don't smile the same
You no longer laugh at the jokes
that once made your stomach ache
You sit and observe
And it hurts to feel this way
You so desperately want to feel happy
You want to enjoy being yourself again
But people have repeatedly destroyed you
You have built these unbreakable walls
that even your loved ones can't access

I was waiting for you to come back
Waiting
And waiting
Until I got tired of waiting
Because if you truly wanted to come back
you would have a while ago

I'm trying to forgive myself for my mistakes—I really am. But it's hard when I've made them back-to-back, ruining whatever happiness I have in my life. Due to my sadness, I push those I love away and invite in dark thoughts that seem to haunt me throughout the day. They especially make themselves comfortable at night, when I stay up and reminisce about the happiness I once had. Sometimes, I feel so hapless because of events that occurred in my life. I know lessons had to be learned, but I know some lessons could have been avoided. Some lessons changed my entire perspective on life. I no longer view it the same—perhaps better—but I view it through yonder lenses. I view life for what it really is; we endure all this pain and depression to die in the end.

Sometimes, love presents itself at the wrong time
And although love makes no mistakes,
Sometimes, loving the wrong person
can be the biggest mistake

Instead of falling in love with you,
I fell in love with my words

I had to take the pain and hide it
To act like I wasn't hurting
Knowing deep down
I was shattering within my own body

You rush your blessings and wonder why things
never fall into place
Please, be patient
Your story is not over yet
There are still chapters waiting to be written

Please, don't give up on me
Understand, some days, I want to stay to myself;
don't want to be bothered,
or just don't feel like talking
I know I won't always show you love,
but trust and believe, I *do* love you
My love isn't always the best,
but it's beyond genuine and real
Don't give up on me, please
I need your strength more than I need my own

I'm so ready to cave back in
Back into my comfort zone, where I know best
Where familiarity comes easy
And my heart doesn't skip a beat at every thought
I want to pry my shell open
and squeeze right back into it
Because I don't know this world that well
And the more I'm in it, the more scared I become
This new world doesn't know my tears
Or how I shut down when I'm overwhelmed
So much to learn
Yet, I can't be the one to teach
Because why would I teach someone
ways to break my heart

I'm so tired of being strong
Having to walk the Earth as if I'm not dying inside
Every day I have to fight these tears
And more nights than most is a losing battle
I don't have it in me to be strong anymore
I just want to look how I feel inside
Maybe then people would leave me alone
Because who would want to bother the dead

If it wasn't for people
I'd probably be truly happy
Wouldn't have to worry about people hurting me
Or why everyone is so weird toward me
Or why I never seem to matter in anyone's life
But when I'm alone
With no one around
It's the music and poetry that keeps me happy
And it's the best feeling in the world
To be in a room by my lonely, captivated by the words
and melodies
Not having to worry about anyone disturbing my peace
Phone completely off
Access to me is dead
Just the way I like it

I'm so tired of being sad
So tired of feeling
Of overthinking
Of existing
Tired of temporary people
And their temporary feelings
Tired of living in black and gray
but having a heart full of color
I'm so, so tired

Be careful when you say you love me
I take love very, very seriously

Maybe someday I'll see my transformation fully
bloom
Until then,
I will keep planting my seeds of growth

I think I love you
And I hate that for me

I'll be proud of myself
When I say "no"
To what was always a "yes"

Maybe, just maybe, life would be easier if I were all *alone*.

There is something about love that I hopelessly dream for, yet I fear I will never receive it. Something about my imagination takes me far into the depths of what it means to love and be loved, yet my imagination is not nearly strong enough to convert my quixotic fantasies into reality. It is almost impossible to grasp. Love is everywhere, yet it's nowhere at the same time. I don't want this new love. The love that comes in the form of betrayal and lust and bitterness. I want the love that doesn't settle. It gives to both of us when there is nothing left to give. I want the love that doesn't exist because this world is too indulged in their own desires to create such a euphoric feeling.

1:26 a.m.

You said you wouldn't hurt me
You lied.
You said you wouldn't leave me
You lied.
You said you loved me
You lied.
You said we were forever
You lied.

Maybe that's why I prefer writing instead of
talking because I know what it's like to be *unheard*

Any girl can give you sex and if that's all you want then I guess
you're satisfied
But when you're finished with her and everything has been
released,
don't go looking for the girl who held you
The girl who wiped your tears
And made sure to pick up the pieces to your crumbling life
The girl you could be transparent with
Or the girl who paused her world to resume yours
Don't forget about her
Don't forget her name
Don't forget her face

I still can't grasp the way you treated me and I, praying you'd do better by me, stayed and waited. I waited for a boy; yes, a boy, who was too afraid to change because he was so enthralled with his old ways. I allowed someone to have me question my worth over and over again, just to discover it was *him* who was never worth it. Time and time again I explained to you how I wanted to be treated and all you said was, *"I'll show you."* You showed me what it means to be loved incorrectly; or to not be loved at all.

I just feel like maybe love isn't for me
I get hurt every time
And I'm tired of acting like nothing ever happened
when I *do* get hurt
Having to rebuild myself and allowing lyrics to explain how I
feel
I love too hard, and I don't think anyone is capable of
loving me more
I overthink, and it just feels like I'm going to lose myself
And as much as I want to be loved…
As much as I want to grow old with someone,
why would I risk getting hurt
Setting myself up for an absolute failure
because I love way too deeply
I want someone for myself
Without having to share with anyone else
Because that's what always happens
And I can't believe I'm loved either
I don't know
Everything hurts

I will not stop asking God to move me; to guide me; to remove those who serve no purpose in my life; to shift me into a better atmosphere. I will continue to ask for strength and wisdom because I'm not always knowledgeable. I will continue to become the woman God has called me to be in this lifetime.

He did exactly what I was afraid of

And more.

I feel like no matter how much love I put out
No matter how much I make people feel loved
No matter how much I tell people I love them
I'll never feel that love in return
And maybe that's okay
to not feel what I'm made of
But it hurts
All the love I have to go around
And no one can spare any for me
No one can make me feel how I make them feel
What did I ever do
Was my duty on Earth to show people love is real
But to never be proven myself

Words.
Words.
Words.
That's all they ever were
Unfinished sentences—
Unfulfilled promises
Words that became lies
Words that never had meaning

There's so much I want to do in life
So much I haven't seen
So many people I haven't met
I want to travel to small towns and sit in diners
I want to see the man-made waterfalls that make my eyes
glow
I want to shake hands with the authors I dreamed of
meeting
Dance with my lover on the dance floor as the song
changes
So many experiences I haven't experienced
So many books I haven't read
So many poems I haven't written
And I *have* to do this
I have to do this before I die

I want the love that never stops loving me. The love I don't have to beg for; or cry for; or reminisce about. I want love that never gives up on us. We work things out, we communicate, we grow. The love that acknowledges all my love languages and more. I don't have to ask for kisses, or flowers, or reassurance, or physical touch. This love understands that when I'm quiet, that's really when I say the most or when I'm loud, I'm not saying it all. The love that God Himself created and molded together. It's love that makes others believe in love. We encourage one another, support one another, build one another. We don't go to sleep angry to wake up upset. It's healthy; it's tranquil; it's simply too good to be true.

It's gonna hurt so much
Might even be impossible to overcome
You'll think about it constantly
To where the thoughts seize your mind
Then one day it won't hurt
It won't happen overnight
Probably won't happen in a year
But one day, one day, the hurt will be over

I used to skip songs that reminded me of you
Now I listen to those same songs unapologetically
Without a trace of you in my mind

I always told myself I'd never fall for anyone like you
again
The pain just isn't worth it
But you were hurting
And I was healing
Maybe I thought I could heal for the both of us
I thought that if I loved you a little stronger,
held you a little longer,
you wouldn't hurt me
But I was wrong
Completely wrong
I saw the signs and ignored them
I welcomed the hurt and allowed you to get me

It hurt so badly to give up on you, but I knew I had to for my sanity. Had I stayed, the tears would have never stopped, and the overthinking would have consumed me. I hope one day in the future you remember my efforts and realize I fought for something single-handedly. I fought for the both of us. I didn't have it in me for any more fights. I'm sorry I had to leave you. I'm sorry I wasn't what you wanted; however, I'm not sorry for making the right decision.

I thank God for the life He's given me. I really, really do. He's provided me with so much. He's put some amazing people in my life and has given me a wonderful personality. I can't thank Him enough. When my mind isn't at ease, God calms me down. When I'm overthinking, God assures me. When I question, God answers. I thank Him for where I am in life and how far I've come. Grateful for everything He's done and appreciative for all He will do.

I had dreams, you know
Of us being happy
Smiling until our cheeks became sore
Embraced in one another's arms
We smiled more in my dreams
We bonded more in my dreams
The dream itself was for us to be happy
How come this only happened in my dreams

Maybe that's my problem. My problem is I want everyone to confide in me. I want to save everyone from their torment and thoughts. I want to hold them as their tears wash them whole and provide them with words of experience. I want to transform their lives, doing everything I can to make it better. I just want to save them. But in the process, who will save me? Who will wipe my tears? Or hold me? Or provide me with words of experience? Who wants to see me become better? Nobody. Nobody wants to listen to my problems or make my life better. I can't save everyone, and Nobody can save me.

I birth so many poems during depression
Maybe my words like me better when I'm sad
They're not used to the happy words
Stick to what we know
I just want to free myself
And create new stanzas
Create a new life
What. Must. I. Do?

I'm not saying we were soulmates or anything
But his body always warmed mine
His hands were always intertwined with mine
Chest to chest, we were rarely far apart
And at one point, he and I were heart to heart

I look back on life sometimes
And I can only laugh
Where I was
Where I am
I don't know the girl who occupied this body
only two years ago
She looks unrecognizable
So fragile. So gullible.
She looks back at me
And there's fire in both our eyes.

I think people prey upon
those with the good hearts
Those with the good souls
They crave that purity in their life
So much so
they'll put on this front
Like they're someone with good intentions
They'll suck you dry until nothing is left
And once they're full,
they leave you
And search for another warm soul

I want to say *welcome* to the woman who came
And *goodbye* to the girl who just left

I feel like I place so much pressure on myself to succeed
To be someone my parents can be proud of
To become someone I can be proud of
Someone for the kids to admire
That I forget the "living" part
I forget to pause
And breathe
And relax
And take life in for what it is
And I don't want that anymore
I want to make mistakes
& take trips out of the country
& laugh with my friends until my stomach hurts
& make stupid decisions that we call memories
So that when I become old and reminisce, I give myself
a reason to smile

The harsh truth I've learned about life is that people may never be as solid as they say they are. I had to learn that most people won't ever be as gentle, as patient, or as caring as me. I had to stop looking for myself in others or I was going to drive myself insane. I realized the same people you fought battles with are the same people to go behind your back and create more battles. I will never understand it. It truly does hurt once people reveal their true nature, but it's the untold truth of life. It's scary. Never knowing anyone's true intentions because their words just aren't enough. Another cruel life lesson I had to learn.

I believe our biggest enemy is time
& that if we don't utilize it enough
it will all be too late
We don't take advantage of it like we should
And that is a mistake we allow to happen too often
It passes us by silently
Creeping through the shadows blissfully
We can't fast-forward it
Nor rewind it
It never stops to tell us what's about to happen
And we never appreciate time
until it's far too late

My heart allowed me
to continue loving those
who were slowly breaking me
I don't know which betrayal was worse
Them…or this heart

You let them in
Y'all bond
Y'all laugh
They leave
Repeat

I often lose myself in my world
One far away from here
Daydreaming endlessly, where tears don't exist
Where I can't feel, but I can live
Reality doesn't exist there
And time is moving at my pace
Everything feels so perfect there
Until
I wake up in the real world
One way too close to me
Dreams abandoned and tears feeling familiar
Where I can't live, but I can feel
A real-life nightmare
And time is moving far too rapidly
I can't stay here

Heartbreaks and memories go hand in hand
Reliving the heartbreak as the days go by
With the haunting memories closing in
Constantly thinking about what was
How it suddenly changed
Then the heartbreak creeps its way in
Like an abandoned soul lost in the woods
Too much pain inflicted on one person
So much anger, tears, isolation
Not knowing who the blame falls upon
And each day, the pain thickens like over-poured
honey

I believe God made me strong
He knew I could defeat the battles
Wither through the storms
There have been so many times
life has broken me into pieces
And God glued me back together
At times, I never quite understood
the reason I endured many things
Until I realized,
I'm an unfinished masterpiece

You invite them in
Hoping they'll be different from the rest
Like a breath of fresh air
After you've been trapped in pollution
But you see the traits
You notice the moods
They're not so much different after all
The same person
Just covered in different skin

After a while, I let my eyes speak
My mouth was too busy swallowing all my words

I began to let the distractions go
The toxicity go
The anger go
And ever since then
My soul has been at peace

In this world full of false hope
heartbreaks
chaos
All I can do is dream

I am more of myself
When I am by myself

I get attached to souls that match mine
but aren't mine
They belong to someone else
But ours paired momentarily
Somehow, I always know they won't stay
I just never know when they'll leave

Words complete me
What my mouth can't say,
my fingers can
Moving rapidly as I spill out my pain from my hand
Writing down all I think of
Hoping it soon makes sense

The silence told me everything I needed to know
I didn't wait for a response
Your eyes said everything you didn't
I didn't wait for words to exit your mouth
It was everything you didn't say
That was everything I needed to hear

I thrive off being alone
I find peace in being alone
I'm much happier when I'm alone
I deserve to be left alone

Sometimes, a chapter in our life must come to an end. And though most times we aren't ready because we've gotten accustomed to the familiarity and the comfort, we must learn to move forward in life. To engage in new opportunities. To meet new people who will bring us peace, laughter and solidarity. It's a huge risk to experience the world from a different perspective, but honestly, these risks welcome new discoveries about us, and we become better individuals.

I'm not sure if it's him I miss
or if I miss the affection
The warmth of a body against mine
Some fingers caressing my hair
The excitement of a notification on my phone
The call I've been waiting for all day
It can't be him I miss
It can't be
Not after he's given me plenty of reasons
As to why I should never miss another again

Just tell me you love me
so that I have a reason to live again

Do not come and disturb me
Do not come and bring weird energy
Keep your evil intentions away from me
I do not have time for weird behavior

There were times when I wasn't sure
what was happening
Everything seemed to be falling apart
and coming together at the same time
Tempted to ask God what was happening
But I knew that whatever He was doing,
it was going to work out in my favor

You didn't see it then
You may not see it now
But one day…
One day you will realize
How much I *loved* you

You were okay with losing me
And I had to learn to be okay with that

Some people come into your life
to show you that your heart is too pure
Your words are too kind
Your touch is too soft
But no matter what,
continue to be gentle
Do not let anyone steal the purity of your soul
The world needs more people like us

To my reader,

Thank you for reading my words. I've always dreamed of publishing a book. Looking back, I don't think my younger self could have imagined I would publish my poetry book at twenty-one; however, I *knew* I would publish a book one day.

Since I was a child, I've always had two desired paths in life; the most aspirational one was to become a writer. I've always dreamed of writing my own books, songs, movies, and plays, but it wasn't until high school that I began writing poetry. I immediately became enthralled with the world of poetry, particularly how the words flowed, rhymed, and provided solace when I needed an escape from reality. Since then, I have been writing poetry. No matter what I do in life, writing will always be the biggest factor. I'm not sure where I would be if I didn't have a connection to words. Writing contributed to my transformation.

I truly hope at least one of my poems resonated with you. I hope genuine emotions were evoked as you turned each page, entering my thoughts and feelings. I look at these poems with a smile now, grateful that I wrote them; grateful that I am no longer that same girl today.

Acknowledgments

To my illustrator, Onur Burc, for bringing my book to life. This cover is absolutely beautiful, and I appreciate you so much for creating it. I will never forget the feeling I had when you first sent it to me.

To my editor, Jessica Berry, for editing my book baby. Because of you, my book is completed, and I am so grateful for you. I knew working with you would be something special.

To my creative team at Ivy Chafin Press. We've worked so hard and this is only the beginning; God is just getting started.

Dejah Freeman

Dejah is an indie author from Ohio who has always had aspirations of becoming an author. While pursuing a Bachelor's in English and Secondary Education and a Master's in English, Dejah still creates time to fulfill her intense passion for writing. Her debut poetry book was released in December 2022, and a year later, Dejah founded Ivy Chafin Press, named after her late grandpa, Ivy, and her late uncle, Joshua Chafin. Dejah attributes all her success and achievements to God as He is the reason she has become the woman she is today. For contact information, please visit www.ivychafinpress.com.

Don't let anyone look down on you because you are young, but set an example for the believers in speech, in conduct, in love, in faith, and in purity.

Timothy 4:12 NIV